SEEING HIS HAND

TELLING MY STORIES AS I REMEMBER

SUSAN D. JACKSON

MESSENGER OF THE GLORY

ISBN: 978-0-578-81174-1

CONTENTS

CONTENTS

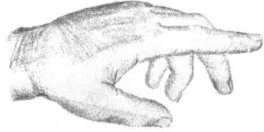

INTRODUCTION

Welcome. I am so glad you are here today reading this book. Will you join me on a little journey as I share with you just some of my true stories where something far beyond me was taking place all around me. Each journey lead back to God and seeing his hand move in my life. I am a very broken person who has made many mistakes in life and am a work in progress like the rest of us but to God that does not matter. He loves me and he loves you too and longs to be a part of our life. Will you open your heart and eyes today to see Him shine in an ordinary person's life?

"Seeing His Hand" is a collection of just some short stories surrounding events in my life that show his supernatural hand from my earliest memories. I called it "Seeing His Hand" because it points the reader to seek to see him for themselves in their own life. I called it "Seeing His Hand," because I have literally seen the actual hand of Jesus pointing at me during an epic battle for my life, so this book is dedicated to my Lord, savior, king, teacher, best friend, and lover of my soul Jesus my Mighty Yeshua. This book addresses the issue in our modern thinking that Jesus is far away sitting in the clouds and has no time for us because he is too busy. This is farthest from the truth! The enemy wants to make people feel lonelier than ever in such a digitally social connected 9 – 5 rat race world. The enemy loves stopping people from glorifying God and sharing time with him. He does not want spiritual eyes to be open to see His hand restoring and healing, developing stories that will ultimately bring God glory as they fulfill what is written about them by God. If the enemy cannot have your soul, he will try to steal God's glory from your life because of you are made in God's image and he does not want your life to bring The Creator glory!

> *So God created mankind in his own image, in the image of God he created them;* male and female he created them.

> — Genesis 1:27 NKJV

Satan hates the image of God and any glory He gets! This book is to reach the saved and non-saved person made in the image of God who is seeking more and to know if God is really so close, if he really cares, and if he will speak to them too. Loneliness can cripple a person's life, and this book will help some to heal, knowing that Jesus is truly all we need, and we are never alone. It will help the reader know they are part of something special and much bigger than themselves.

This book presents many benefits besides the simple mission to give God glory with my stories and will address many people in many different seasons of life, even touching them at a crossroads.

1. Someone thinking of abortion will be able to have

their eyes open to the fact babies are real people from day one in the womb because of my memories in the womb.

2. People who are struggling through losses of jobs, divorce, homes, and provisions will be moved to know that God is with them and has not forgotten them or their needs. He is a loving Father of provision and strategy.

3. The reader, who may someday have a demonic encounter and won't know what to do as a Christian and wonder why such is happening, will be empowered.

4. The reader will understand angels are assigned to help each and every one of us, in turn shining more truth of the love of the Father who really does care about our daily lives and crossroad events.

5. The reader will learn the importance of inviting Jesus not just devotional times but also in the busyness of life and treating him as the real person he is and realize he too has feelings.

6. A new level of relationship will develop between the reader and their maker (for those open to it) after reading this book as the book helps to heal old wounds, answer some questions, and bridge the gap between their negative feelings and the reality of God's ever-present love.

7. Readers will realize the importance of what they speak and the power of the tongue.

8. The book will simply give God all the glory in the stories leaving the reader to fall in love with him even more!

This book is dedicated to my heavenly Father and to all the lives who are somehow part of these stories and to my heavenly angels who have assisted a stubborn person like me my whole life. It is also dedicated to you the reader who is made in His beautiful image.
I want to give a special thank you to my husband and friends who pushed me to continue my writing when life hit me hard at times.

CHAPTER 1

FIRST LIFE

TELLING MY STORY AS I REMEMBER

*T*otal darkness consumed me. My first memory was just a state of being. But as I grew, I came to discover I could do more. For some reason, although science and logic would say no, it is not possible, but with God, all things are possible, I have memories of being in the womb. My first memory is tough to describe. On this side of life, I will try my very best to explain it to you.

I had the ultimate state of just being in the beginning. There was limited understanding present in me. I could think and reason in its simplest form with the ability to think about questions as time went on. I understood the English language. Probably supernaturally because that is the language I would speak when I was born. Each stage of development, I was aware. At first, it seemed I had plenty of space, but with time, the space I had known became harder and harder to move within it. I already had emotions. Whenever I felt fear, an angel attended me. That was the nursery angel.

As time went on, I became aware that I was inside of someone. The nursery angel tried to help me understand, but I still did not grasp it. However, at some point, I began to hear noises on the outside. Hearing unclearly, I could always make out the voices, music, and loud abrupt noises. I could even feel when my mom was upset, which happened numerous times while I was in the womb. Each time that happened, the emotion of worry would grip me. If I did not cry out to the angel every so often, they would appear any way to check on me. When they would come to me, within the womb, I would see a supernatural bright light to the top right-hand corner of me. That is where I would see the face of the loving, gentle being each time they came.

Curiosity began to grow, and I felt a stronger presence behind the angel that I wanted to know, but they did not allow me to. I would press the angel often to know more about them and where they came from, wanting at times to not be left alone and go with them. I wanted so strongly to know the one who sent the angel, being fully aware someone else was in control, but who?

With a feeling of being left out, I would get upset and wanted more of what was on the other side of the angel than knowing more of what was outside the only home I ever knew to this point. These days, I know it is God. Time passed. I began to see with my eyes. Within the daytime, I could see a reddish glow coming from the outside walls of my mother's tummy. At nighttime, it would get dark, and I would notice the activity outside would settle down. I did not know what daytime or nighttime was. I had no concept. I just grew to know that a cycle of some sort would repeat. I remember hearing music. I remember hearing when my mom would be upset with someone, and it would scare me. Memories of her emotions and how they affected me are so very real.

As more time went on, it seemed my atmosphere grew smaller and smaller. And let me tell you to remember those painful growing pains you experienced as a child or teenager, babies in the womb feel that too. I remember starting to feel pain in my growth, but I did not realize I was growing until one day I noticed something growing out of my sides slowly day by day that I could wiggle, and those wiggles grew more control. I remember the first time realizing I finally had hands and what I could do with them. I was in awe.

Snug tightly, I was desiring not to feel that way anymore but feeling safe in this place, it was all I knew. Continued visits from the nursery angel continued until one day, it seemed everything changed.

"I have an important message for you," says the angel. "There will be changes soon. These changes must take place. But do not worry, we will help you get ready."

I was thinking of changes. Strangely, I understood what the word 'changes' meant already supernaturally. If there ever was something I was confused about, the angel would help me understand better and work with me.

"Soon, you will be leaving what you have known. You will be born."

I asked the angel, "what does it mean to be born" and although they explained several times at my request, I still was at a state of partial understanding. Yet, once full realization hit me that I would be leaving all I knew, fear of all the unknown hit me. The angel did their absolute best to reassure me everything would be well, and I would not be alone. I am sure they spent many days getting me ready for what was to come.

Then the day arrived. The nursery angel gave me my final instructions. "You need to go toward the light. When you see it, keep moving toward the light and go along with the flow of the pulling."

"*What!* I thought, *how terrifying!*" I remember arguing with the angel and pleading. They finally had a heart to heart talk with me.

"If you do not go, the two more to come cannot come."

I asked what that meant.

They repeated it. "If you do not go, the two more to come cannot come."

They repeated that sentence to me over and over every time I pleaded no. Finally, I sat still in the silence and thought about what the angel said. Suddenly, in my heart, I knew there were more like me, and somehow, I was connected to the two more to come. My heart hurt that they could not have a chance to be where I was. I felt as if I should move on and let them come. I ended up having two baby brothers in the years after my birth.

I told the angel, "Okay. I will do this you're asking."

Not much more time passed, and the moment arrived. I had changed my mind. I struggled with the nursery angel over this. But then suddenly something else happened I had not known.

The nursery angel left me, saying, "Someone else is coming to take my place."

Suddenly, another angel was there, and this one's presence was still safe but not as kind and gentle as I had always known. This one was the one to give me the firmer guidance I needed throughout the birth process.

In this life, I have been very stubborn. It is no surprise to me that I was assigned a kind and loving yet aggressively effective angel. My memories of him seem to me now as if he was like a coach meaning well but, at times, pushing you hard emotionally to get you to the finish line. In my natural stubbornness, he was who I needed.

"You are going to feel tightness like you have never felt yet. When you see the light go toward it, do not stop. If you stop, it will end your life and your mom's."

I was thinking, *"Mom? Is that the name of who I've been with all this time?"* I felt instant pain in my heart. I did not want to hurt this mom, but I did not want to leave safety. I was terrified.

"Do not be afraid. I will be with you. When you get out there, you will see me. You will hear the sound of your voice. I will need you to just cry and let out your air when you leave here and enter the light. At first, it will hurt and be painful, but it will only last a moment then be over. The light you will see will also hurt for a moment."

I was counting on what the angel promised me and that the pain I would endure would not last long. I was counting on his promise that I would see him with me on the other side. So, with determination, I finally let my stubborn will up. I knew I must go so the two more to come could do just that, and so I would not hurt Mom.

Years later, I found out that my mom was, in fact, near a dangerous death giving birth to me. I had gotten afraid one last time while the angel coached me, and I stopped moving toward the light. The pain of the tightness was so uncomfortable. I cried to the angel to help me. I could not move. He then proceeded to give me the final push I needed to accomplish moving on. The rest of the journey was easier, and I was moving forward fine. My mom explained all these years later that I had gotten stuck, and no matter what they did, they could not get me out. She was also suffering from deadly toxin levels; they were afraid if I was not born soon, they would lose her. So, my choice to go forward indeed saved my mom's life and the life of my future brothers who were to come. God gave me a choice but also assisted in guiding me to his perfect will. He knows our hearts, even from the beginning, and knew I did not want to cause harm to the flow of what was to happen. I was only afraid.

So, the moment happened, and I saw the light larger than ever and went for it with all my might, and in an instant, I hear a pop, and the pain hit me like never before! The light he warned me about that would hurt was very true. He had also warned me the world would be cold. Indeed, it was when I exited the warmth of my mom's womb. I felt hands handling my body, and it felt strange; I did not like the lack of control. Yet I also was able to stretch for the first time, and that felt wonderful. I remember fully the moment I was born once I saw the doctor's face after the glaring bright light hit me. I rolled my eyes as I was crying out loud, scaring myself with my own cries, to see the angel in the corner of the room. We communicated without me speaking.

I said in my thoughts, "Where are you?"

He said, "I am here."

"Where," I asked.

"Look over here."

And there he was indeed with a bright large consuming light behind him. I felt he was not alone.

He said to me, "I have to go now."

"Please, no, you said you would be with me."

"Yes, I will always be with you." And like that, he was gone.

I cried so much out loud, hoping for him to reappear. This encounter I had once I was born lasted only a few seconds our time. I cried in my spirit and my real-life lungs for him to come back. I was scared.

I proceeded to hear laughing and the angel's voice speaking with someone, and all I heard was, "I told you she was a tuff one."

And just like that, I saw him again. I said,

"I want to always see you. I need you with me."

The angel said, "You will not always see me, but I will be there. We will be there. All you have to do is call for us."

And with that, I saw him give me the warmest smile he had ever given me in our brief encounter that made me realize he was not so bad after all. I knew he and I would go on to know each other my whole life and be connected. Knowing he meant what he said, I let him go as I continued crying with my scared uncertain outlook of this new place. I saw the large bright light he had stepped out of close up behind him as he turned to walk away with the others behind him that I could not make out. I felt left out but knew, for now, this new place I found myself in was where I was supposed to be whether I liked it or not.

How does this message apply to you? Here is a message for you that God wants you to know.

1. God is indeed our Father—creator. Psalm 139:14
    "*I will praise you; for I am fearfully and wonderfully*

made: marvelous are your works; and that my soul knows right well."

2. God knew you before you knew him. Jeremiah 1:5 "Before I formed you in the womb I knew you before you were born, I set you apart; I appointed you as a prophet to the nations."

3. Your life is no mistake nor anyone else's. Isaiah 44:2 "This is what the Lord says, he who made you, who formed you in the womb, and who will help you. Before you ever arrived in your mother's womb, you were indeed in the thoughts of God. God has plans for your life."

4. Every single baby born has a purpose. Jeremiah 29:11, "For I know the plans I have for you," declares the Lord, "plans to prosper you and not to harm you, plans to give you hope and a future. Ephesians 1:4 "For he chose us in him before the creation of the world."

5. There is a book written about you. There is a book written about your life in heaven; that's how special you are to him. Psalms 139:16 Your eyes saw my unformed body, all the days ordained for me were written in your book before one of them came to be. Wow!

If you are considering abortion, just know the baby knows you already and can feel the pain no matter what you have heard at young stages. I felt pain in the womb even if it was growing pains. The baby has emotions. The baby has a purpose, and it is not for you to decide if it lives or dies, but that is only God's choice. If you are pregnant and scared, please seek help. We make mistakes BUT God does not HE redeems our mistakes and can turn them into some of the world's biggest miracles. If you have had an abortion God is ready to heal your heart tenderly but forgive yourself

CHAPTER 2

THE ANGEL AND THE SUITCASE

*E*verything was wobbling as I tried to have a steady hand. I was playing with a few small toys, but with the motion and bumps, it was a challenge for my tiny toddler hands. The up, down, back and forth (as I rode in the back of the covered pickup truck) was so much fun this particular day in the late 70s. This was before the days of seat belt laws and required seating. Those were the good old days! You could go down just about any street seeing a mountain of teenagers or kids riding without seats in the back of an uncovered pickup truck, feeling free as the wind blew past at high speeds. No seat belts, are you kidding me? That is any three-year old's dream! I enjoyed playing on the truck bed's cold floor under one of those 1970s hard truck cover shells as we drove 700 miles from upstate New York visiting family. This, to me, was a total adventure.

On this particular day, I remember hearing my mom and dad discuss, "Next time we take a trip to New York, maybe we should bolt some seats into the back of the truck."

I thought, *"no! I hope they forget to do this awful thing! It will end all my unrestrained fun."*

To a toddler being left in the back of a pickup while parents were on the other side of a sliding window with no way to discipline, this was a nice arrangement. Unless they stopped the truck, and my Dad never wanted to stop the truck except for gas or lunch out of the Coleman cooler. He was a man on a road trip mission with no slowing down. With this in mind, I felt grown up in my newfound freedom. The trip seemed long to a preschooler with a short attention span, but I knew how to keep myself busy. The swaying of the truck bed continued along our journey.

I peeked into the little slide window in the middle of the truck and said for the hundredth time, "Are we there yet?"

"No," Mom said, "we are not there yet, so sit down like I told you!"

But I liked poking my head in the window to see what was going on and annoy them a tiny bit, knowing Dad would not stop the truck. I was a very bright toddler.

"Mom, I am hungry!" I learned on the trips when I would say I was hungry; I got as many snacks as I wanted if I persisted, unlike at home. "Mommy, can I have a snack?"

"No, you just had one."

"But Mommy, I want some of those cheese crackers you are eating."

"Ok, here ya go. Now sit down."

I think she shared them with me to hush me up. Victory! *"These cheese crackers and Mountain Dew are so yummy,"* I thought to myself as I slowly nibbled at them.

But in an instant, everything changed. *"What is that scary loud sound, why am I being surrounded with this bright light, and who is this person picking me up?"*

"MOMMY! Where are you, MOMMY?

It is so bright. Why am I being thrown? What's happening?" I felt someone with me. "Who are you? Mommy, where are you? It feels so tight in here." I was so scared, but why did I feel so warm and safe? What was the very bright light that consumed me?

"Do not be afraid," a voice said.

Why did this voice and presence seem so familiar like we had met before, yet it all seemed so odd and unfamiliar at the same time?

"Why am I so tight and curled up with no way to move? I feel icky."

I heard, "Wait. It will not be long. You are safe."

"But Mister, let me out of here."

"Not yet, but it will not be long."

"But I want my mommy now," I protested.

"You will see her soon." His voice seemed so reassuring to me, yet it was beginning to seem like forever.

So, scared I was but also feeling safe remaining curled up tight with tears slowly quietly running down my face. I knew whoever was with me was there to help me. It was now dark, I thought my mystery keeper had left me, and my fear grew.

I said, "Where are you?"

This game of hide and seek was strange to me. His bright light and presence were back in an instant, and I felt comforted for a few moments. He had always been there; I did not always see him.

I was silent, trying to hear what was going on outside where I was to figure out my situation. It became dark again. The nice man was strangely still with me, but I could not see his light anymore. He began to give me instructions.

He said, "You need to cry hard and to keep crying loud."

"Why, Mister?" I asked.

"So, they can find you," he stated.

I didn't understand any of this. I started to cry, as I missed my mom. I started moaning louder as the comforting voice in the dark prompted me. "Keep crying."

So, I did. I thought it was strange that I was told to keep crying when my whole life adults would rush to my aid to quiet me.

"Now, when you see the light, do not be afraid of a man who will find you."

In an instant vision, I saw what the man would look like; the helper had shown me.

The helper said, "Keep crying louder."

So, I did, and in a few more moments, I heard a man's voice.

"She is over here," I heard him shouting.

I eagerly cried louder as I heard noises, and voices grew louder out here. In a moment, I saw a sliver of daylight that then began to grow.

I listened to the man say, "You're going to be ok, little girl."

Then I saw full sunlight. The darkness and tightness was gone! I saw the face of the same man the helper had shown me moments before, so I was not scared and leaped up into his arms, trustingly. I heard a roar of cheers and saw a lot of faces when emerging, alarming me. I clung to the man in his arms for dear life. I refused to let him go until I saw my mommy or dad.

The man said, "Little one, you must go with this lady. She will help you and take care of you," as the female EMS worker was walking up.

I said, "No. I want to stay with you." I did not like the looks of her, and she didn't look like the man who helped me. I cried with all my might looking in the sea of faces for my mommy as I clung to the woman. Then all of a sudden, I saw my step dad. I leaped into his arms, feeling safe again.

I heard my dad yell to an ambulance, "Tell her she's been found alive."

In an instant, the ambulance drove away in a furry. I knew in my tiny young mind something bad had just happened. I didn't know what and something was wrong. Mom was in that ambulance. I did not know if I would ever see her again. Dad reassured me that mom would be ok. Years later, I found out that she refused to go until I was found alive, although she was medically in grave danger. He proceeded to pass me back to the strange lady to watch over me until my Aunt Roro from North Carolina arrived. Then dad went to join my mom wherever she was. I sat for what seemed like an eternity in a cold, starlit office with this lady. She asked me if I would like to eat. I was in silence and stunned by the day's events, and I finally asked for cheese crackers and mountain dew. I was thinking, I was upset. I wasted my snack in the truck big time by now. Oh, how the mind of a three-year-old works!

You see, they found me in one of those blue hard-shell suitcases that were so popular back in the day that had a built-in lock. I had overheard my dad saying earlier that day at the crash site, "You found her where?"

The rescuers answered, "the blue suitcase."

Dad said, "That's impossible! I had it locked. The key is in my pocket."

"We found her locked inside," the rescuers replied.

The suitcase protected me. They found it lying in the rubble of twisted metal and glass that surely would have killed me. Back then in New York, my uncle would save glass soda bottles for us to bring back to North Carolina for money. There was a lot of glass in the back of the truck with me that day. Now I know in my adult years the bright light man was an angel. I did not know back then what an angel was, although I had previous encounters with them that, at that time, I had forgotten. In an instant, he threw me into the suitcase to save my life. Had he not supernaturally thrown me in the locked suitcase, I would not have survived the glass and bed of metal my suitcase cocoon was laying in.

How does this miracle apply to you? Here is a message for you that God wants you to know.

1. You are made in the image of God almighty. There are over 17 verses in the Bible, pointing to God making us in his image. Genesis 1:26-27 is the very first one. Then God said, *"Let us make mankind in our image, in our likeness, so that they may rule over the fish on the sea and the birds in the sky, over the livestock and all the wild animals, and over all the creatures that move along the ground."*

2. God assigns angels to assist us. According to Psalms 91:11 *For he will command his angels concerning you to guard you in all your ways.* If it weren't for the angel's swift obedience to God to assist me, I would not be here today to tell you this story to bring God the glory.

3. Everything in creation points back to the glory of God. If you are wondering why you are here, one of your main missions in life, first before all others, is to live in fellowship with him and give him glory with your life, as you cooperate with the plans he already has for you according to Jeremiah 29:11. *"For I know the plans I have for you," declares the Lord, "plans to prosper you and not to harm you, plans to give you a hope and a future."* You will begin to see the supernatural assistance in your life, knowing it is God's loving touch on you. As you see his movement, tell others, as you give his image glory through you for you are made in his image. Never take this lightly.

4. Once you come to faith in Jesus and what he did for you, you have access for the rest of your life to heaven's protection and provision. Hebrews 1:14 *Are not all angels ministering spirits sent to serve those who will inherit salvation?* Indeed, they are, and they are ready to assist you today.

CHAPTER 3

FOUR DEMONS
WHO LOST

a s a young 20-something mom with a preschooler and a baby on the way, you need all the sleep you can get. Those days I could sleep deeply at the drop of a pin, I would be so overwhelmed and tired. It was not normal for me to wake so suddenly.

Awakened with a jolt from a particularly good sound sleep, I looked right by my side and saw nothing but darkness, moonlight, and the faint glow of the alarm clock numbers. Realizing I had just been woken from sleep, my blurry eyes were coming into focus. As my eyes adjusted, I was stunned at what I saw.

Peering into the moonlit room, I saw four tall, dark figures in dark hooded cloaks. Thinking for sure I was still asleep at this point and was possibly dreaming, I turned my head to the large digital alarm clock on the bedside again to see what time it was. Seeing the red glowing number flip over to the next new minute, I knew then I was not asleep.

With my heart pounding, I turned to see if I still saw the four dark figures surrounding me as I was in a daze of utter confusion. Indeed, the scariest, most demonic things

I had ever seen stood around me. There was one standing at the corner of each of my feet and one on each side of my side. I was struggling to see their faces, but I could not see them. They, like cowards, kept their faces hidden in the deep, vast darkness behind their hooded garments. I am glad I could not see the faces for fear of what it might be. I saw boney no-flesh hands and fingers like a Halloween skeleton. The boney hands reaching past their long, dark bell-shaped sleeves into me and ripping relentlessly. With each grab, they spoke the most slanderous mean words I had ever heard coming at me in my entire life. They cursed at me and promised, with each violent word, they would indeed kill me. I noticed I felt the beginnings of ripping pain into my body that was like nothing I had felt before. I felt like someone was sticking long, fat needles dipped into rubbing alcohol straight through my body at every square inch.

I thought to myself, *"there is no way this can possibly be happening to me because I am a child of God, and things like this do not happen to children of God how dare them!"* Realizing as each second passed, my spirit was rising out of my body. I could feel it before I could see it. Once I got just a few inches above my body, they ripped harder and continued the horrible speech towards me and insults and continuous death threats. I was shocked my body was laying flat on the bed as my spirit hovered above.

I tried moving only to find I was paralyzed. Fighting hard to turn my head and yell for help, only to no success. The air was slowly leaving from my lungs as my spirit tried to yell out for help. No one heard. The demons let me know it was no use as no one would hear me. Then they paralyzed my head and neck, so at that point, the only thing I could do was move my eyes. Looking forward to the dark ceiling was really all I could do. Rolling my eyes to see the figures, I was being assaulted over and over. This was my reality.

Feeling death closer and closer was terrifying at this point. I was at the end of desperation. *"Where is my Jesus?"* I waited for Jesus, but he did not come. For sure, in this unreal horror movie moment of my life, he would super-naturally show up! He didn't.

In my heart, I said, *"Jesus, why have you forsaken me?"*

I waited for a response. Nothing… Looking at the four demonic punks killing me, I was feeling more helpless than I ever felt before in my life.

I decided to try again.

"Jesus, why have you forsaken me?"

I kept thinking it and saying it with my very soul. It was the only thing the demons could not take control of—my thoughts. But each time, the demonic beings seemed to get stronger, louder, more forceful. They knew what I was thinking in my spirit. They knew I thought Jesus had aban-doned me and loved that I believed so. The more fear I had, the more power they displayed. Demons feed on fear and lack of faith.

You see, where there is a lack of faith, the opposite will happen; it is all a chain reaction. Everything in heaven functions on a legal realm. Faith is literally a shield. And where there is none, you legally have given your circum-stance to the enemy. So, demons don't even have to guess what you're thinking. The lack of faith and what it produces says it all, and they love it. You either have faith, or you don't. I said it one more time and was so very sad in my heart. I was about to die without my Jesus to save me, who I believed would always be there with me. I was already thinking when I got to heaven, I would ask him,

"What the heck? Why didn't you save me back there? Why were you punishing me? Why, Jesus, did you leave me all alone?"

Now, do you see how fickle I was? I was thinking I had faith. Yet in the same breath, I was saying, "Why, Jesus, have you forsaken me?" That in itself is not a display of faith.

As the torment persisted, so did my lack of faith. I continued to think in my heart, "Jesus, why have you forsaken me?" Then suddenly, right in direct sight of my eyes above my head to the right, a very tiny pure-as-a-diamond light appeared. All I could move was my eyes, but that is all I needed at that moment. I thought, *"wow this is it. Jesus has finally come to rescue me!* I was thinking, *ok, demons; this is it. Get ready for a throwdown."*

The tiny Diamond light was like no other light on earth can produce. It was so pure. With the vast darkness around me, it certainly stood out. The tiny light grew, and it was about the size of a baseball when it finally started opening. Looking in amazement and wonder, I saw a pure white mist within it, that at this point was hovering right over my head. Surely this was a peek into heaven? I saw the outline of a face looking down through it at me. Stunned, I was hopeful it was Jesus.

I said, "Jesus, why is this happening? Why have you forsaken me?"

I saw this misty figure lean in a bit more from the outline of a large throne, and what seemed a very large hand with a finger pointing was coming towards my face. If it wasn't for the present torment I was currently enduring, I would say it almost looked comical—that big hand. Then just a few inches from my spirit's face, it stopped.

I stared at the finger pointing at me, and a voice with such sternness and authority came. It sounded like when a parent is disciplining their teenager or child. He almost sounded annoyed yet firm.

He spoke these simple words, "I have not forsaken you!"

I was thinking, *"then why on earth am I here in this position right now?"*

He knew exactly what I was thinking. He said it again, "I have not forsaken you."

I was thinking, *"then why are you not saving me from this torment?"*

He said it once more very firmly and direct, a bit louder. "I have not forsaken you!"

Then he sat back on the throne, and the hand drew back upwards into the light, and the portal closed up. It totally vanished in an instant, leaving me bewildered and alone.

That was it. That was all he said. Five words were all he spoke, and yes, at this point, I was certain it was Jesus. I was very grateful he did indeed show up yet also baffled at the fact He was gone, and I was still suffering. I was upset. I felt hurt in my heart. I was just disciplined by Jesus in the middle of my demonic torment. If I didn't feel loneliness beforehand, it was worse than ever now. All of this, from start to finish, only happened in a matter of minutes, but this whole ordeal seemed like forever and that it would never end. I was left by Jesus in a state of confusion in the middle of my demonic torment.

I was lying there still floating above my body, thinking how to get out of this. Let me think logical here and see if there was some key point I was missing. I was grasping at straws. I realized Jesus did not save me from this fight but I started to get this funny feeling maybe, just maybe, I was missing something. I started to replay in my mind what Jesus had said.

He said, "I have not forsaken you."

Ok, what was I missing there? Jesus had gone, and the demons were still here, and Jesus had not gotten rid of them for me. I repeated in my mind again, *Jesus has not forsaken me.* I said it again, looking for the clue.

Then it started to hit me slowly; then, it hit hard. I thought, *"just because Jesus did not save me from the battle doesn't mean he had forsaken me".* I started to change what I was repeating and saying to myself. *"Jesus has not forsaken me."* Point blank believing each time with more faith as I said it. Jesus did indeed show up, and I know he responded to me with a loving, firm message for a reason. His showing up had to prove he had not forgotten me. I truly believed this now at that point without any doubt.

As I kept saying as loudly in my spirit as I could, "Jesus has not forsaken me. Jesus has not forsaken me," and growing in my faith, I noticed a shift in the demons' behavior. They became, if it was even possible, more aggravated and annoyed. It seemed they heard me loud and clear in the spirit and was responding to the revelation I was now declaring. They actually started to sound arrogantly fearful of what I was saying. The more I said my rant to them and myself of "Jesus has not forsaken me," my faith arose. At this point, they began to lose grip on me little by little.

As I chose to believe what I was saying, their grip matched my level of faith. I find that interesting. The more I said it, my voice became louder and no longer weak in paralyzation. More of my control of my body and my spirit came back. You see, my spirit was only a few inches above my body. I was not dead. My soul and body were still connected, so every bit of what I would tell my body to do in the spirit, my physical body would respond (when I was not paralyzed) and could feel the pain the demons had inflicted throughout the whole ordeal.

They began to shrink as well as continuing to lose their power. Their rips at my body became not as painful. The nasty hate speech that was once loud was sounding lower in volume, and it got to a point they sounded like whispers I could barely hear the more I declared by faith Jesus had not forsaken me. Before I knew it, inch by inch, the demons shrank to literally the size of a childhood cartoon character.

Although they still had me paralyzed, I could move my neck and head at this point. I turned my head to see them running around in circles. It was almost comical, and my faith was now real faith. I finally had enough, and while they ran in circles, I could hear chipmunk sounding words of hate speech. Yes, their voices got very small. I knew at this point my fear and lack of faith are what this type of demon had been feeding on to grow. The more I professed my faith in Jesus and what he already, note I said already, did for me at the cross to them, the more they lost their control over me.

I said in one final bold fully-believing-by-faith shouting in my spirit as I turned to look at them, "Jesus has not forsaken me. Now go in Jesus name!"

Poof! Just like that, they vanished and all that remained for a few minor seconds was four little tiny puff clouds of smoke. Gone. Now at the second they left, my still hovering spirit slammed back into my body with a powerful thud. Yep, it went thud. It hurt so badly! My whole body hurt for over a week due to this! I realized there is such a strong connection with your spirit and body while on earth, and they affect each other in ways most do not even realize. The demonic attack was over. Jesus, by the power of his blood at the cross, already saved me. I had just learned how to tap into that and use the authority he gave me in him.

How does this message apply to you? Here is a message for you that God wants you to know.

Jesus' message for you today is to have faith like a little child knowing once you have asked him to wash your sin away, and you give him access to your heart forever, he will indeed help you in all situations. Even if that is teaching you how to walk out your faith and defeat a demon by faith in his blood and name. Jesus has not left us defenseless. He has given us the word of God. Let us look at how to equip you to also defeat a demon.

1. Put on the armor of God. Ephesians 6: 10-18
    The Whole Armor of God *10 Finally, my brethren, be strong in the Lord and in the power of His might. 11 Put on the whole armor of God, that you may be able to stand against the wiles of the devil. 12 For we do not wrestle against flesh and blood, but against principalities, against powers, against the rulers of the darkness of this age, against spiritual hosts of wickedness in the heavenly places. 13 Therefore take up the whole armor of God, that you may be able to withstand in the evil day, and having done all, to stand.14 Stand therefore, having girded your waist with truth, having put on the breastplate of righteousness, 15 and having shod your feet with the preparation of the gospel of peace; 16 above all, taking the shield of faith with which you will be able to quench all the fiery darts of the wicked one. 17 And take the helmet of salvation, and the sword of the Spirit, which is the word of God;*

18 praying always with all prayer and supplication in the Spirit, being watchful to this end with all perseverance and supplication for all the saints—

Seriously do it daily. Not only do you need to put it on, but you need to walk in it. It will do you no good unless you walk it out and live it. Walking by faith is the activation. Using the Sword of the Spirit is how Jesus himself defeated the devil in the desert when he was tempted, I believe partly as an example for us. Whenever the devil came to speak temptations to him, Jesus response was always the word of God. He would use that sword of the spirit to cut the enemy away every single time, and he would flee. Look at Matthew 4 in the Bible for his perfect example.

2. Your citizenship is indeed Heaven. According to Philippians 3:20, Our citizenship is in heaven, from which we eagerly wait for the Savior, Lord Jesus Christ. But while we live on Earth, we do have the help all of heaven provides, and that is accessed by your faith. Ephesians 2:4-6 *But God, who is rich in mercy, because of His great love with which He loved us, even when we were dead in trespasses, made us alive together with Christ (by grace you have been saved), and raised us up together, and made us sit together in the heavenly places in Christ Jesus.*

3. Miracles can happen by our faith in him. Remember the words of Jesus in Matthew 17:20 *So Jesus said to them, "Because of your unbelief; for assuredly, I say to you, if you have faith as a mustard seed, you will say to this mountain, 'Move from here to there,' and it will move; and nothing will be impossible for you.*

4. Faith MUST be bigger than your fear. It is

normal for us to struggle with a measure of lack in something but remember, do not let your fears and doubts be BIGGER than your faith because then you will get what you fear. Also, do not make an idol of your fear or worry. Only God deserves our constant thoughts and deserves to be God. A lot of us make our fears, worries, disbelief an idol before God not even realizing! You can, through the mighty power of Jesus, move mountains and walk in the authority of Jesus, knowing who you are in Christ Jesus.

CHAPTER 4

SUPERNATURAL PROVISION

Story one: He Owns It All

I looked in my wallet to see just how much money I had left till my next gig to make some money. I found seven dollars. As a single mom with two small kids and no one to help me, money was hard to come by. I could not afford daycare or babysitters so I could work. I had to work on the weekends when the kids went to see their dad every other weekend and find ways to make money with them during the week, such as babysitting. These were the days before work at home telecommute options.

The Lord had been stirring in my heart about giving and tithing. I used to tithe when I was married. The Lord was saying to me, "What about now?" Pondering I had to remember all the times he supplied enough to meet needs when I was married.

But this was different. I was no longer married and did not have the help of a husband. "Do I give now?" I wondered.

Exploring and weighing this, I realized yes. Although I already knew the answer in my heart after the Holy Spirit reminded me of the Bible story about the widow and the mite in Mark 12:41-44, Luke 21:1-4 I should have known better and trusted the word of God.

He reminded me in my spirit and in the word that all belongs to him, including my seven dollars. There are many verses on this. For example,

> The earth is the Lord's, and everything in it, the world, and all who live in it.
>
> — PSALM 24:1 NIV

for, "The earth is the Lord's, and everything in it"

The Bible declares over and over in countless verses in scripture that everything belongs to God. When I finally made peace with that, I felt that God say even your last seven dollars.

"So, what now God? Do you want me to give you my last seven dollars?"

I felt this was what he wanted. As fear started to fill my heart, I remembered hearing once evangelist Joyce Meyer say, "Obey God even if afraid, just do it afraid." But I also remembered this from scripture at the same time that God loves a cheerful giver. I wanted to bless the Lord's heart by showing him I trusted Him since it all belongs to him anyway.

> Remember this: Whoever sows sparingly will also reap sparingly, and whoever sows generously will also reap generously. 7 Each of you should give what you have decided in your heart to give, not reluctantly or under

compulsion, for God loves a cheerful giver. 8 And God is able to bless you abundantly, so that in all things at all times, having all that you need, you will abound in every good work.

— 2 CORINTHIANS 9: 6-8 NIV

So, I had resolved the next time the church doors opened, I would throw my full seven dollars in the basket at tithe time even if I was afraid. I needed to be careful to give with more joy than fear.

Then the day came. The worship that day was special. As I worshipped, I also pondered giving the Lord all of my seven dollars. At the same time, I wondered how I would make ends meet, but I gave up again, knowing my God is bigger and owns it all.

The worship continued softly as the Pastor announced, "Let's continue the worship of our God by presenting to him your tithes and offerings."

My heart started to race fast with a mix of emotions. I was sweating as my heart thumped in my chest. *"I can do this. I will do this for you, Jesus. You own it all."*

I walked forward to the front of the church, holding my seven dollars tightly, and knelt at the tithe basket. I was sniffling at this point and said, "Jesus, this is for you; you own it all" as I threw my last bit of cash in the basket.

Trembling, I got up and walked away praising God, knowing there was no turning back. I raised my hands, praising God, relieved actually that it was now in his hands, not mine.

As I got back to my seat, I said, "God, you own it all, so take care of us."

Raising my hands in worship with my eyes closed, I cried and worshipped him. When service was over, I felt so alone, yet I still knew God was with me. It is a strange thing to experience when you know what is to come, but you must contend with life here on earth. I gathered my little ones up to get ready to go. This was a new church we had not been going to for too long. Not everyone knew my name, but I smiled at people and hugged necks, and made small talk on the way out the door.

Suddenly, a little old lady with such a sweet smile said a few sweet words. To this day, I cannot remember what they were. She also handed me a piece of paper. I thought that it was awesome to get a note of encouragement. I had been singing praise once before, and a younger teenager had given me a note saying how they loved hearing me sing. I thought that this would be something like that. I wanted something to look forward to later, so I thanked her and hugged her neck as I placed it in my pocket.

Once I got the kids all buckled up in the car, I was sitting there looking at my children's faces wondering what next. Should we go home? Should we ride just a bit for fun? I knew they would be hungry for lunch, and I really could not afford to waste gas. I was so sad that I had no money to even take them to McDonald's for a kid's meal while they got to play in the indoor kids' gym. In those days, there was nothing much to do in that small town for kids other than that. For a moment, I said to myself, "God, I feel so alone and forgotten. Ya know what, I am going to read that note now before I even start this car." I felt I really needed it. I opened it and in the piece of paper was $70 dollars. Total shock took me over and relief at the same time. How did this lady I did not know, know? Only the Holy Spirit of God knew. Before I even left the building that day, God had taken care of me.

Story two: The Dress That Made Me Cry

"The kids are gone to their dads for the weekend; what will I do Friday night," I was thinking. I was feeling a little sorry for myself all alone. When you are married for years, then all of a sudden that is gone, it is such a hard adjustment. I missed going to the mall and walking around, feeling a part of society. I thought, *"I do not need anyone to go with me to have a good time; I will go and walk with Jesus"*. I said, "Jesus, do you want to go on a date with me today?" I thought, *"good, let's do this."*

I arrived and began walking and taking in all the sights and sounds that I loved about a mall and it was something to go and do and not feel so alone. A tiny part of me still was feeling sorry for myself. Every step, I felt alone yet not alone as I talked internally with the Lord. I praised him when I did not see a way that day. I welcomed him to walk with me. I talked and talked some more. After a while, I went inside of a clothing store to look at clothes. I thought, "why *not? Jesus might enjoy it too. I do not have the money to buy a dress, but the Lord and I can look."*

As I looked at clothing, a dress really caught my eye. I thought, *"well, the word says God owns it all, and if Jesus wants me to have a new dress, he will provide in his time."* But these beautiful things were just so pretty, and I thought, "why *not just try them on and play dress up."*

I was standing in the dressing room now looking at myself in the mirror, crying as a tear rolled down my weary cheek, feeling sorry for myself that I was alone and had no money to buy the dress. Suddenly, something broke in my heart. *"I am not alone. I have been talking to Jesus yet still living in the sense today that I am so alone with no money to boot."* I thought deeply of the Lord and felt he was a little sad. I said, "Oh, Lord, I am so sorry to be more focused on my heart rather than yours. You are here, you are really here. I will continue to try on these dresses and do it JUST for you, not even for me."

So, as I looked at the dress that caught my eye on myself, a little rush of joy came over my battle-worn heart. I began to twirl in that dressing room, before the Lord as I watched the beautiful dress flowing, turning in childlike circles. I did it several times and said, "Lord, this is for you; you are worth twirling for!"

On the drive back home that night, I thought of the evening and felt better and fuller. I also thought of my kids and how I wish I could go to the market and buy the snacks they used to enjoy, but sometimes snacks were hard to buy when watching every penny. When I was married, I could afford the snacks they really wanted.

As I thought about these things, I shook it off and drifted in my thoughts to believing God would supply, and I left it at that. I had not even prayed to ask God for the things my heart desired that night.

The evening went on, and I found myself sitting in front of the computer reading and doing anything I could to keep busy and from allowing any more feelings of loneliness overtake my heart. I resolved I was not alone and felt contentment in the evening when all of a sudden, the doorbell rang to my surprise! I was not expecting anyone. I also lived in a neighborhood that was not the best and opening my door for anyone after dark I did not know could prove a bad move.

I went to the door and said, "Hi, can I help you," and a faintly familiar voice was behind the door. I opened it, and a sweet teenage girl stood there with a box. Her mom had driven her there to deliver this box to me. I was shocked. I did not know them very well, but they attended the church

I was visiting. My thoughts were of shock; first, how did they find me, and secondly, "what *were they doing here?*"

I said, "Oh! Hi, Kendra, what are you doing here? Do you want to come in?"

"No, mom is in the car. She just brought me to bring this to you."

I was shocked again. I took the box and said, "Do you want me to open it now?"

"No! Open it when I leave. Mom is ready to get back home."

I hugged her and thanked her and waved at the mom.

Walking back inside, trembling, and as tears already hit my eyes, I was in wonder. Just the thought of being remembered when I struggled that day with loneliness was a huge blessing. Yet, what was in the box?

As I opened it, every snack I had desired in my heart for my kids that they used to love but I could not afford was in that box even though I had not asked God for them. But he knows what we need or want! There was also THE DRESS. The same dress, just like the one I had tried on in the store hours before, laid before me brand new in the box. I burst in full tears in amazement. How did they know? There was no way; only the Holy Spirit of God knew. At that moment, any traces of loneliness that may have been lingering left as I felt so tenderly loved and cared for by my Abba Father. I went to put on my dress for my Abba as I was praising him with warm tears of gratefulness running down.

Story three: Christmas Miracle

A knot was in my stomach as thoughts of Christmas were haunting me. Christmas was only days away, and I had no gifts for the children. Money was hard to come by in between odd jobs to make ends meet. Being single and not being able to afford daycare traps your ability to make more money. I missed the days when I was married, and we could afford to buy the children gifts. My son was used to getting a few nice things during the holidays. My daughter was still too young to know or remember. These are my babies, and I want to spoil them some!

As the day went on and the activities, the business with the kids grew, but even in the midst of the busy, thoughts still loomed about the lack of gifts. You would've thought by now all the incredible things God had done to provide for me, I would have dwelled on the assurance he would take care of me. I knew he would but then again, maybe not this time.

Whenever I thought of gifts, I imagined at least a doll for my girl and a remote control car for my son would be nice. Yet still, I do not remember praying for it specifically to God. Well, later in the week, on a day that I was feeling particularly sorry for myself and the kids, I decided, *NO. No more! I will trust God has us*

Now, the kids and I were having a great time chatting up a storm in the car coming home. The Holy Spirit of God dropped something in my heart like, "Prepare to be amazed." I was thinking, *"wow, is he about to do something?"* I just knew before I arrived home a miracle was about to happen. I had already prepared my son and baby girl this holiday might not look like other ones we had before due to mommy being short on cash. My son had been taught about Christmas being Jesus' birthday, not ours, the year before. Yet, I think he still thought Santa came.

So, as we approached home, I felt led to look on my porch as I was approaching from the street. "*I see something, but what could it be*," I thought?

"Look! There is something!"

I helped the kids get unbuckled from their car seats, and we ran up on the porch together. There was a paper bag that felt heavy. We took it inside the house. There were two wrapped gifts. My son was so excited. I kind of wished he had not seen them because I could have placed them under the tree for Christmas morning. He asked me who the gifts were from. I said they were from Jesus with such excitement in my voice and heart! I told him Jesus left the gifts for him and his sister!

"Wow, Mom."

I said, "Let's thank Jesus."

And we did!

So, I was hoping he would not want to open it. But it was inevitable.

"Mom, can we open it now?"

I felt joy in my heart to say yes since he had a tuff year. He opened it, and what do you guess was inside? It was a remote-control car! My baby girl opened hers, and it was a doll. Exactly what my heart had desired to give my kids, but I had not even asked God specifically for those. I just knew he would take care of us, but this time he knew the desire of my heart. I searched frantically in the bag and the wrapping paper for a note of who it was from. There was no note anywhere. To this day, I believe Jesus sent an angel to drop those off on our porch. What joy it brought.

Story four: The Toddler Bed

So, when I had moved into the house on the wrong side of the tracks all I had for my toddler was her crib. The kids and I in those days, would browse Toys R Us for fun and often I would desire the while toddler bed they had for sale for my baby girl. Well one morning I felt the Lord saying, "get in the car now!" I was shocked. It was early and cold outside. But I felt such a strong pull to go. So, I obeyed and bundled up the kids and we took off for a ride. I had no idea where we where going. I just drove where I felt led to go. We drove into a neighborhood many miles away I had never been to. I turned down many streets with no personal plan other than following where I felt led. In my heart I felt as if I was going after my toddler bed I kept seeing it in my spirit! Sure, enough on the final turn what do I see by the road? The very same white toddler bed I wanted from Toys R Us! It was on the curb being thrown out! Moments behind me was the trash truck. I had just beat it to my blessing by literally seconds.

How do these miracles of God's provision apply to you? Here is a message for you that God wants you to know.

1. There are hundreds of verses in God's word that tell of his love for you. Go and see. Here is one to get you started. Romans 5:8 *But God demonstrates his own love for us in this: While we were still sinners, Christ died for us.*
2. He will always take care of you, just believe. Psalm 37:25 *I was young and now I am old, yet I have never seen the righteous forsaken or their children begging bread. What YOU must do is simply believe and have faith in him to provide.* Hebrews 11:6 *And without faith it is impossible to please God, because anyone who comes to him*

must believe that he exists and that he rewards those who earnestly seek him.

3. Do you know this God and that he knows you? God supplied my kids a gift. I had not even told God what I wanted; he already knew my thoughts. Now I do not say this to say we should not pray; that is not it at all. I am saying God knows YOU. He certainly knows you and your needs and cares about each and every one of them.

CHAPTER 5

COMMANDING ANGEL'S

*M*y heart was beating fast as we drove back towards home a day after Hurricane Floyd. Not knowing what we would find along the way. The storm sent mass destruction everywhere in my city. My body and mind were completely utterly exhausted, not only from the storm, but I had a 4-year-old and a newborn baby born just two weeks prior to the hurricane. Flowing floodwaters grew by the minute.

I settled in the back seat after buckling the kids in their car seats. Keeping an eye on my little ones as we drove, gazing out the window at what looked like an apocalyptic dream. My ex-husband was driving. We were stunned at all we saw. We encountered flooding all around and would have to find other ways to get home. After rerouting a few times already, we were approaching a couple of miles near home when we spotted yet another flooded area that was growing too fast. My husband was approaching it as I looked in disbelief the closer, we got. The road we needed to continue on was blocked by the rising floodwaters. We had seen some people trying in other areas of shallow flooding, attempting to go through

37

it by car to get home. Some cars were being swept away in the waters current in other areas. I did not want that to be us.

"Hey, you're not going to go through that, are you? Oh no! Please, don't go through that; it is rising too fast," I pleaded.

I was so scared at this point. His patience trying to find yet another route home was gone. I began to pray to ask God's help as we began to drive into the water.

As we attempted driving, the water was rising fast. It was a large area. The strong force of the current pushed the car. My heart was pounding with such fear it gripped my bones. Suddenly, the car stopped. The engine was underwater that fast. Water was starting to pour into the car. The water on the outside of the car was almost up to my passenger window. Terrified, I unbuckled my four-year-old son and put him in the back-window ledge of the back seat. I unbuckled my newborn baby and held her up, so water does not get to her. I was so afraid and did not know what to do to save my babies. I could not swim or open the door due to the pressure of water on the other side. My husband just sat silently in shock not moving. Our windows could not roll down in the back due to child safety features.

"Mommy, what's happening?"

I tried calming my son down, but inside I was terrified.

"Stay there, son." I began to panic, yet in that moment, all I had was my faith as my legs were beginning to get wet from the rising water.

I cried out loud to God to save us. I cried out loud in the name of Jesus.

As I was crying out for help from the Lord with the most urgency I had ever had to that point in my life, the car was being tugged by the current. Still no answers.

Suddenly, I heard the Lord's soft yet strong voice in my spirit say, "You command the angels."

Immediately I knew what I must do. I said, "Angels of God, come now and help us in Jesus' name."

Now at this point, the engine was too far underwater to start. The back end was starting to sway with the current. Immediately I felt the car jolt as I was hearing the sound of metal rubbing and squealing. The back end of the car rose up as if something big was picking it up! I turned to look, and I could not see the angels, but I felt two large angels had taken hold of the back bumper and picked up the back end of the car! I knew it and felt them.

My son said, "Mommy, who is that?"

He sensed it too, and I said, "Wave at the angels, they are helping us out of here!" I was amazed and relieved as I sat raised up off the ground in the back seat.

I was in shock as the car was now going against the current straight and forward towards safety! The Angels not only picked up the back end where the children and I were, but they were pushing the car forward against the current.

I heard the Lord gently say, "Tell your husband to start the car."

I was shocked and said back, "But car engines cannot start underwater."

I heard it again, "Tell your husband to start the engine."

So I shouted, "The Lord is saying start the engine.

He said, "It is impossible."

I said it again, begging him to obey what I heard. I said one last time, "The Lord thy God said, start the car."

I knew the Lord was wanting to show himself strong to my husband. So I said it loudly one more time, and he finally turned the key. The car started! Since this event, I have gone to countless mechanics to ask if a car engine can start in the water. The answer is no.

As the car was still rolling forward, our eyes were big with shock. I was so grateful. At this point, water was getting pretty deep inside the car. And when a car is in a situation like that, the water is higher outside the car than inside at first. All of this situation happens in only a matter of moments.

As we got onto dry land with each roll out of the water, the angels started to lower the back end of the car down to the ground. When it finally set flat to the ground, I heard the metal all rub and bump as they placed us down! I sat with my heart about to fall out of my chest at the event that just happened. My son and I waved at the angels and yelled, "thank you" to them and God with tears running down my face.

I learned so much in that miracle encounter. There were other times I know without doubt angels attended to me and helped me. There were even times, for example, I forgot where I left my keys, and I would be on a time pinch, only to feel inspired to look in a certain place and find them after calling on my angel to help me. Whereas on my own, I was in a hurried rush and having no success. The angels saved my bacon many times in more ways than one. I highly suggest calling on angels of God to help you in sticky situations! God has indeed assigned them to you.

How does this message apply to you? Here is a message for you that God wants you to know.

1. Do you want to know how to get to God? Just believe in his perfect son, who he sent to die for your sins. John 3:16 *for God so loved the world that he gave his only begotten son, that whoever believes in Him should not perish but have everlasting life.* He made it that simple, but we tend to complicate it. We all are born sinners into a fallen world, but he made a way to get us back home. Accept his son Jesus today and call on his name to come to wash your heart and be your savior. He is waiting.

2. Your citizenship is indeed Heaven. According to Philippians 3:20, *Our citizenship is in heaven, from which we eagerly wait for the Savior, Lord Jesus Christ. But while we live on Earth we do have the help all of heaven provides and that is accessed by your faith.* Ephesians 2:4-6 *But God, who is rich in mercy, because of His great love with which He loved us, even when we were dead in trespasses, made us alive together with Christ (by grace you have been saved), and raised us up together, and made us sit together in the heavenly places in Christ Jesus.*

3. His angels are assigned to help you. Psalm 91:11 *For He shall give His angels charge over you, To keep you in all your ways.* Hebrews 1:14 *Are not all angels ministering spirits sent to serve those who will inherit salvation?*

4. We are made in his image. Genesis 1:27 *So God created man in His own image; in the image of God He created him; male and female He created them.* God created the earth and all that is in it by speaking it; just look in Genesis. Proverbs 18:21 *Death and life are in the power of the tongue, And those who love it will*

eat its fruit. So just as God spoke life and good things, so can we.

5. God wants us to obey what he says to do. John 14:15 *If you love me, keep my commands.* Other translations say, *obey me.* And in the instant, I was calling out to him, he gave me instructions. He said to me, "Command the angels."

God sent His son to save your soul, not the angels. 1 Corinthians 6:3 *Do you not know that we shall judge angels?*

CHAPTER 6

DATE NIGHT WITH JESUS

$\mathcal{T}$he house was bustling with noise from teenagers, as a sudden thought came to me. As I worked on kitchen duties, I realized, I had not invited the Lord on a date in a while. So, I set out to change that.

"Lord, tomorrow at 6 pm, I would like you to join me on a date," I declared to him.

I was drumming up the plan in my mind to dress up extra special for him, intending fully to make it happen. I was unclear about what we would do for the date but incredibly determined in my heart that it would happen. Excitement fluttered my heart. *"What would Jesus and I do,"* I asked myself and envisioned us sitting in a comfy coffee shop or on a park bench, watching people over a cup of chai latte tea. I knew he would lay on my heart what he would like to do, and that was fine by me.

Washing yet another dish at dinner time the next day, a gentle yet urgent reminder came to my thoughts. I had a date with Jesus at 6:00 pm. It was after dinner time the next day by this point. Why in the world did I make a date with Jesus at dinner time when I was the one that cooks the family meals?

The cell phone said 6:10 pm. Returning to wash dishes, a guilty feeling settles over me. I justified in my mind that if I did not do kitchen duty, no one else would. I could easily have my date with Jesus after completing the tasks.

Suddenly, a still small voice said, "What about me?"

Rinsing the dish, I pushed past it thinking it was just me making it up. I heard it again in my spirit and with it, a feeling from the sender of heartfelt disappointment. Then, it dawned on me. "Is this dish I am holding more important than my Savior?" Immediately I wiped my hands and ran upstairs.

"Oh Lord, I am so sorry." I got spruced up, sang, and chanted, "I'm going on a date with Jesus."

The night before, I had been thinking about writing a love letter to Jesus. So, I announced to everyone downstairs, "I'm going on a date with Jesus; try to keep it down."

The apartment we lived in at the time was unique. My third-floor bedroom upstairs was a loft where every noise in the house rose from the two floors below me. Grabbing a blanket, I made a tent to go into alone with Yeshua. Next, clutching a clipboard, I prepared it for writing. Lastly, I put on some instrumental worship music flowing through my headphones. I did not want worship music where someone else was singing. I wanted all possible focus on the Lord.

"Jesus, here I am. I am deeply sorry for being so late my Lord, and for treating you as second fiddle to chores. You are far more important than anything in this world. Jesus, I do not know what to do on this date with you other than start writing a love letter from my heart to you."

So, I began writing, and words of love and adoration just poured from my pen. Pausing often, I would think about him. More words came faster than my pen could move about how I felt about my best friend. Shutting my eyes to pause again, something extraordinary happened, something I was not expecting. Seeing with my eyes closed, in my spirit, the Lord was sitting on a large rock on the edge of a beach. He was smiling at me. I thought this was too good to be true. "*I am such a mess up. Why would Jesus make time for me? This must be my imagination.*" Quickly, I opened my eyes. Thinking about what I just saw, "*wow, that felt and seemed so real and much more apparent than my imagination.*" I started writing back, and soon after, I paused again to ponder the Lord.

Closing my eyes instantly, the crystal-clear vision of Jesus was back, and he was smiling at me. Immediately my thought was, I sure wish I could be closer. Without fail, like a movie camera zooming in closer, he brought my viewpoint nearer to him. Before that, he was quite a few feet away. Jesus drew me into his space automatically. He knew my thoughts without me saying a word. He was still smiling the most amazingly warm smile I had ever seen. I was wondering, "*why is he on this rock sitting sideways with his feet pointing west?*" I also noticed the reddish-orange light of the sun setting across his face. At one point, it got so bright.

Opening my eyes to disbelief and awe of what I was experiencing, I sat amazed. Thinking again, "*is this my imagination?*" I thought it could not be. I was not doing any thinking but just experiencing. With a pleasantly stunned heart and tears flowing, I began writing again. Soon stopping to close my eyes once more instantly, he was still waiting on me, and he had me back in the same place. I felt so unworthy to be in the presence of the King. Noticing from the corner of my eye, I could tell the ocean was crashing extremely hard as if a storm was coming. I tried to look, but my eyes were fixed on him. I tried several times to look at the crashing waves, but he kept my face locked on him. I did for an instant look down at the sand as well as my feet, but on my view back up, I tried stubbornly to look at the waves. He refused to allow it, but all the while, he was still smiling at me, and I kept my eyes on him. It struck me as odd, but I knew somehow, he was teaching me something deep in my heart.

Glancing one last time at him, I opened my eyes, yet again in disbelief this was happening. Closing my eyes again, this time he was gone. No matter how many times I would close my eyes, he was gone. Then in amazement, I sat thinking about what just happened and that indeed the experience was not my imagination. He allowed me to see him three times, which is the Biblical sign of confirmation.

Crying, I began attempting to write, with tears hitting the page. Why did this happen to me? What was Jesus saying to me even though he never spoke a word? Feeling like a fool, I wished repeatedly I had not opened my eyes and had just spent more precious time with him. But with a tear-stained paper, I continued writing him my letter with a renewed purpose. Then I just sat, listening to the music remembering his smile and reliving it in my heart.

How does this miracle apply to you? Here is a message for you that God wants you to know.

1. Sometimes we make commitments that mean well at the time, but then life happens all too easy. Why do people go on dates seeking the perfect companion but never make time to set a special date with Jesus officially? Now I'm not talking about your typical devotional time with the Lord. Those times are indeed special, but most times

end up being a prayer list. But do we ever set a
time to give to him and find out how he is feeling?
He is indeed ready to tell you when you ask and
listen. This life offers many things, many joys to
embrace and cherish. Yet even in what the world
can offer, the soul longs for more. It seems nothing
or no one can fill the void, only the one called
Jesus, who indeed has feelings too. Yet, we do not
tend to invite him to outings and more.

2. Imagine for a moment you're waiting for a date
   whom you care for deeply, but they forget to come
   to pick you up. The date goes on ahead and
   enjoys the date without you as they run into
   mutual friends while out. As they socialize and
   have fun, they totally forget you're sitting at home,
   waiting to have fun as well. That would stink. I
   feel like sometimes Jesus feels this way about his
   bride, YOU!

3. What are some feelings a person might feel in the
   above example? Left out, sadness, longing,
   loneliness? There are many other emotions one
   can feel, but these are some I am almost positive
   the Lord feels at times when we forget to make
   space for him. God created us for fellowship. He
   spoke so much in that one encounter, to not only
   me but you as well. I know for a fact, by the smile
   on his face, he was happy that I made time to seek
   him in this new way. He will be pleased if you do
   this with him as well, and it does not have to be
   exactly how I did it. Matter of fact, I want to
   make this a lifestyle of inviting Jesus everywhere.
   Even when I drive alone, I clear the passenger seat
   and tell Jesus to come to sit and ride.

Ya know what? Here is a mini testimony. I was listening to the radio, and that same voice that reminded me of the date I had set with him said to me, "Turn the radio off. I would rather listen to you sing." I knew he was there as I drove and sang to him. To think had I not made a date with Jesus, I would've missed what he had to say that night I saw him on the beach. Here is what he was saying to me and YOU when I saw him on the beach.

How does this miracle apply to you? Here is a message for you that God wants you to know.

1. In troubled times, our focus should not be the problems, but our focus should be on the solution, and his name is Jesus. That was why he would not allow me to look at the violently crashing waves but kept my focus on him.

2. Time is running out for us to do what we are called to do. As the sun set on his face, it was to remind us that time is almost up. Go love your neighbor today. Do not wait. Whatever it is you know God's calling you to do, get it done. I also believe the sun setting means he's coming soon.

3. He was on the rock also to remind us all, he is the rock and sure foundation. Matthew 7:24-27. 24 *"Therefore whoever hears these sayings of Mine, and does them, I will liken him to a wise man who built his house on the rock: 25 and the rain descended, the floods came, and the winds blew and beat on that house; and it did not fall, for it was founded on the rock. 26 "But everyone who hears these sayings of Mine, and does not do them, will be like a foolish man who built his house on the sand: 27 and the rain descended, the floods came, and the winds blew and beat on that house; and it fell. And great was its fall."* So, what are you building upon? Is it Jesus or sinking sand in which you build upon?

4. Jesus was on the rock to remind us he is the cornerstone, and without him, there is no proper support to the foundation on which you build. He calls us to believe in Him. Isaiah 28:16 *Therefore thus says the Lord GOD: "Behold, I lay in Zion a stone for a foundation, A tried stone, a precious cornerstone, a sure foundation; Whoever believes will not act hastily.* Also, Luke 6: 46-49 *"But why do you call Me "Lord, Lord," and not do the things which I say? Whoever comes to Me, and hears My sayings and does them, I will show you whom he is like: He is like a man building a house, who dug deep and laid the foundation on the rock. And when the flood arose, the stream beat vehemently against that house and could not shake it, for it was founded on the rock. But he who heard and did nothing is like a man who built a house on the earth without a foundation, against which the stream beat vehemently; and immediately it fell. And the ruin of that house was great."*

CHAPTER 7

THE BLOOD WALL OF JESUS

*L*ife was full of disappointments under trails mixed with blessings as well. But as anxiety was yet again hitting my heart, mind, and body (trying to lure me to worry), I said to myself,

"No, there has to be a better way."

This life is hard in this fallen world. Indeed, it is, with so many things coming at us internally and externally. Stress and worry is the name of modern life, and if not dealt with, it will grow to be a monster choking out your life. To combat this, I like to listen to the testimonies of others who have dealt with a messy life and how they overcame. I happened to be listening one night as I waited for sleep to Sid Roth's program. He had interviewed Evangelist Billye Brim. Her family was being assaulted by the enemy, as she ministered to God's people. She told how to "build a blood wall of Jesus," and she did it, and she saw changes.

"So, is this amazing or what? I have to try this and will do it every day," I thought to myself. So, the next morning, I got up, and before my feet could hit the ground, I did what Dr. Billye Brim said. I said it with a sound of authority coming

from my voice, out loud. You see, the devil is the prince of the air right now, so you must say it (not pray it) out loud. Also, go back to Genesis in the Bible and see that God spoke the world and all creation. He made us in his image (Gen. 1:27) He made us creative beings in his image. With that in mind, he also said in his Word there is power and death in the tongue (Proverbs 18:21). You can create with your tongue good or bad, and it is honored in the spirit realm.

So, as you build the blood wall, you must speak it so the enemy actually sees it even if your physical eye does not. I said, "Satan, I am seated in Heavenly places with Christ Jesus, (Eph. 2:6), and you are not; therefore, I put right now a blood wall of Jesus between you and me. And I went on down the line praying for each of my family members, building the blood wall in the same manner as I had faith it was there and seeing it in my spirit man imagination as I went along. I continued doing this for months and did not tell a soul. Only God and I knew.

But one day, I was in a lack of faith moment and said, "Father, is it really there?"

The Lord knows we struggle at times, and he has been gracious to me whenever I have wanted confirmation.

A couple of weeks passed, and my son, who was a grown man by this time, came to me and said, "Mom, my girl-friend (his girlfriend at the time but now wife) saw something that scared her, and I am wondering what it was to try and help her."

I said, "Tell me everything you know that she saw." As he proceeded to tell me, I said, "I know exactly what that is," as I laughed with excitement! I said, "Let's take her to lunch, and I will chat with her myself."

SUSAN D. JACKSON

She was laying in her bed and saw a dark demonic figure coming towards her, but when it would try to touch her, a swirly blood-like substance popped up and prevented the being from getting to her.

I told her, "that is the blood wall of Jesus I have been speaking into place around you every day now for months."

Wow! God opened her eyes for a moment to see the reality of what was going on. What I had been speaking with authority out loud daily was working! God is amazing! His son Jesus Christ mighty Yeshua's blood is amazing. God did not leave us in this world all alone and defenseless. He has given us tools and using faith, our mouth, and his son's name and blood will help you in these trying days. I build the blood wall daily around my family and call them each by name because people sin and choose wrong at times, which lowers the protection, and the Lord is a gentleman and will not force us to abide in him. He lets you choose who you will partner with—him or the enemy and your flesh. It is a moment by moment choice until we get home.

How does this message apply to you? Here is a message for you that God wants you to know.

1. Hebrews 11:1 *Now faith is the [a]substance of things hoped for, the [b]evidence of things not seen.* Faith is all about totally and simply believing something without even yet seeing it. I did not see the blood wall I speak daily around my family but as I speak it out loud into the air I TURST it is there because I know as it is written in Matthew 19: 26 *But Jesus looked at them and said to them, "With men this is impossible, but with God all things are possible." And God was gracious to me to give evidence that indeed what I spoke out loud in faith was there.*

2. God formed the world by speaking it as it records in Genesis of the Bible. He also made man in his image. Genesis 1:27 *So God created man in His own image; in the image of God He created him; male and female He created them.* He made us co-creators as well. There is power in what you speak into the air that profoundly affects the unseen realm. If you speak curses over someone or even have negative self-talk guess what you get? If you speak life over something, someone, or yourself you get life. Proverbs 18: 21 *Death and life are in the power of the tongue.* That sound wave emits through the air with more power than you realize. **Will you use your voice wisely and co-create life around you? Your voice matters to the seen world and unseen.** Proverbs 12:18 *There is one who speaks like the piercings of a sword.* But the tongue of the wise *promotes* health.

CHAPTER 8

**THE HOUSE OF
RESTORATION**

any hours passed while worry had gripped my soul. I had called everywhere looking for my husband, but he was nowhere to be found. Every thought imaginable crossed my mind as I prayed. Holding my baby girl in the recliner, he finally walked in and said, the words no young bride with children ever wants to hear.

From that moment on, I lived the worst fears and pain imaginable. Fear of what will happen to me and my then very young children gripped the deepest parts of my heart night and day. I will spare you all the painful details of what happened next, and the spiral downward our lives had become and all the poor choices we both made.

Months had passed, I drove to what I thought would be our family home forever. It was the home I had to flee due to the emotional turbulence I kept enduring. I ran anywhere someone would take me in for a short seasons only. I had hoped that when I arrived back, that things with him had changed. Upon my arrival, I noticed the locks on the doors had been changed. All of our belongings were in the house, and I had no way of getting my stuff or the kids' stuff.

Slowly with my heart in utter agony I pulled out of the driveway crushed, I could no longer look at my home. But what I did look at for what seemed like forever was my mailbox as I exited the driveway. That image was burned in my heart of my black mailbox. "God, why, I do not understand what is happening? I do not want this for us, God." As tears streamed down my face, his gentle spirit impressed into my heart and mind Joel 2:25. I hung on to that promise as I drove away, looking at my mailbox in the rearview window, knowing that would be the last time I ever saw it. The house number was 209.

A few years passed, and I remarried. We bought my current husband's first home, (post leaving the cruise industry). It was a cute little colonial cape cod style home. It even had a white picket fence and a colonial-style courtyard. With him being from New England, this house was a perfect fit for both of us. It went on to be our home for seven years. The house number of this home was 107. This is also important for you to remember for later.

Hearing the nearby church bells ringing every day gave me peace at times of uncertainty and boy did we hit many. The trees in our yard were a source of comfort as I would sit outside and pray, in all of life's seasons. One of my favorite parts of this little home was the ornate white mantel on the fireplace. Every season the mantle was carefully decorated with love. The mantle was the first thing any visitor could see walking into the tiny house, and I wanted it to be welcoming.

After many years in that home raising children, my husband felt it was time to move. The town we lived in had no jobs and was ridden with crime. We moved to a new city with a new start of hope for a better future for us all. The day we left our house, we cried. I heard the church bells ring that last day before moving and said, "God, I know in you, all things are possible. Please may my future home have church bells that ring nearby." Leaning on my beloved mantel and touching it, I also said, "God and I want a mantel just like this one in my future house." Proceeding to touch the focal wall behind it, "Lord, and I want my walls to be this color of gray." The Father truly hears everything we say, even if we think something and do not pray for it. He hears your prayers and sees what desires are in your heart. He truly delights to see us smile.

So fast forward seven years bittersweet years later to our life in Raleigh. When we moved to Raleigh, we rented an apartment for the first few years. Desiring to be in a home, I would take walks in the cute older neighborhood a few streets over from our complex. Then the Lord opened a door for us to rent a home in that very neighborhood for a few years, and it was a great home and fulfilled the need for a house, but it was not our home since we did not own it. In those years, there were many great moments and trials of many kinds in the apartment and rental house. The kids also grew up and moved on. As grateful as we were to be out of the apartments and into our cozy brick rental home, it was time to move.

With the rent increases in the area, we pondered that a monthly mortgage payment is a lot less. However, during those years in Raleigh, my husband experienced many job setbacks and job changes.

We were still in a recovery phase financially when my husband said, "We are not renting anymore. We are buying."

I said, "Are you nuts? We simply cannot afford that right now" or so I thought. But as I know, God can do anything he wants to do.

"Susan, I am just too busy at work to go look at homes. You know what I like and what we are looking for in a neighborhood, so you go. And if you like the home, then I will go to see it."

"But, I have already been to 20 plus homes, and I am tired and frustrated. I am not going to anymore unless you come with me."

"Suzie, I simply do not have time, and there is a house you have to go see. Just this one last time." So reluctantly, I looked online at what he was talking about and decided I would drive out to see it.

Now prior to my husband coming across this particular house, I had been frustrated and stood in the driveway of the last home I had been to see and said, "God is it possible to get us a home that is two stories, near or part of Raleigh, on a cul de sac, with trees, etc." My list went on with what my husband would have wanted and I. Now before my husband saw this 'final house,' something else extraordinary happen. We had been driving down the road, and I was whispering to Jesus, "Where is my home?" In an instant, I saw a clear vision flash that lasted three seconds. In the narrow vision, I saw beautiful pencil trees. I saw white porch railings. And as I glanced down, I saw natural wood planks. Then poof, it was gone. It startled me in a delightful way. I told my husband it seemed I just saw part of our new house.

So, the day came when I went to see the house after my husband saying, "Let's have the faith of a mustard seed." I was happy he felt led to have this challenge because the numbers were indeed impossible. The home was being sold on a new house selling app called Open Door. I could go walk in the house without a realtor when I entered a code. If the home panned out, then we would call a realtor.

The day came, and I went to see the home. I was driving and praying, *"Lord, let your will be done. Wow! Look at this long driveway and the two pretty little dogwoods on each side at the entrance."* It was a beautiful home, but it seemed like it would be out of our league.

I walked onto the porch, and as I was fumbling to enter the code on the door, I felt the holy spirit say, "Turn around."

I stopped what I was doing and turned around only for my gaze of sight to fall on the same narrow vision of what I saw two weeks prior. I was in shock as I checked each detail with my memory.

"This can't be happening?"

I walked into the living room of the house to discover the entry was exactly how I would want it. I turned to go into the living room, and there, standing before me, is the same mantle I had asked the Lord for, but this time it had marble instead of brick as I had secretly hoped but never prayed. I walked around, and the walls were all the same shade of gray I had wanted. The living room had lots of windows as I had wanted. I went to the back porch, and what did I see? A hot tub! It was not in the home listing. The desire of my husband for so long was to own a hot tub. *"What is happening here?"* I wanted at least one room with a vaulted ceiling. The master bedroom had the vaulted ceiling! Side kitchen door was in—check. Laundry room under the stairs—check. Front porch to sit on—check. Shop out back with electricity. Check. Trees for my husband—check! This house was everything we wanted and was a part of an unincorporated area that would eventually belong to Raleigh.

So, as I was leaving, I sat at the end of the driveway staring at the mailbox. I was unsure. Thinking to myself, "this *house is too good to be true, and I will not get my hopes up.*" Well, as I sat and pondered talking to God, I looked at the mailbox, and it seemed familiar. Why? *"Oh, I know why; I used to own a black mailbox like this almost 20 years ago."* But that was not it. *"Why am I sitting here Lord, looking at this mailbox."*

Then I heard his voice say, "I told you I would restore the years the locust had eaten."

Then my memory opened up, and I instantly remembered the image of my black mailbox burned in my memory as I drove away. Then I thought, *"wait a minute."* My daughter was now 19 and I had been in prayer for her life for years as she struggled desperately in many areas. The Lord reminded me her nickname I had given her when she was a baby and it happen to be 'sweet pea.' The house I was sitting at was 209 Sweet Pea Lane at the end of a cul de sac.

I started crying like a newborn baby. "Lord, is this mine? Is this house what you're giving me?"

Somehow, I knew in my heart this was indeed my house. It was a fulfilled promise of restoration, and not only that, but it was also a sign he would restore my daughter to his original plans for her life too!

Driving away crying worse than the raindrops pouring outside, my heart was so touched and tender with thoughts of, *"is this happening?"* But doubt came in. I went home to the apartment, and my husband said he would go see it.

The moment he drove up, he said, "This is our house." He had not even seen it fully yet. He just knew. As I ran around, showing him everything with excitement, he said, "Let's get it."

It took at that stage in our life a financial miracle. But everything fell into place for the home to become ours after two weeks of speaking life into it even when the realtor said someone had already gotten it. That in itself was a miracle of God. But the story is not over yet. Remember our house we cried when we left my hometown at 107 and the church bells I listened to that day and told God I wanted them again?

During the home buying process, we had land surveyors come out. I came one day to check behind them. I opened up my map to look only to discover my house of 209 Sweet Pea Lane was sitting on lot 107! I was blown away in awe.

Moving day came, and as the final box was loaded into my new house, the moving truck pulled out. I walked back towards my house and heard a beautiful familiar sound of home. I heard church bells ringing so well, coming from a nearby church. I had not heard church bells ring in 7 years.

I stood crying.

"Lord, how is this possible!" I walked into my house to lean on the white wooden mantle as I did the day I cried at house 107, asking for the same mantle and church bells to ring daily on the hour. I leaned on it in honor of that prayer 7 years before.

As the days went by, I realized the year that my new house was built was the same year my divorce was final, and I lost my home. WOW!

How does this message apply to you? Here is a message for you that God wants you to know.

1. God truly is a God who cares for every single detail that concerns you. Jeremiah 29:11 11 *For I know the thoughts that I think toward you, says the Lord, thoughts of peace and not of evil, to give you a future and a hope.*

2. God is a God of restoration. Joel 2:25 25 *"So I will restore to you the years that the swarming locust has eaten, the crawling locust meaning your choices, people who have harmed you or the devil himself.*

3. God has not forgotten about you or your pain. Deuteronomy 31:6 *6 Be strong and of good courage; do not fear nor be afraid of them; for the Lord your God, He is the One who goes with you. He will not leave you nor forsake you."*

4. He indeed honors faith of a mustard seed. Matthew 17:20 *So Jesus said to them, "Because of your [a]unbelief; for assuredly, I say to you, if you have faith as a mustard seed, you will say to this.*

5. Forgiveness is key. God made a way for us all who are sinners to come back to him through his son's perfect redemptive blood. If God will forgive you, how much more will he expect that of us. And it is so healthy for you inside. Trust me, if I had not forgiven my ex, myself, and the past, I probably would not be in my house of restoration today. Look at the story in God's word in Matthew 18:21-35.

CHAPTER 9

RIGHT NOW

*S*o, do you feel alone, like God is so very far away? I think, at times, we all feel that way to different degrees. Do you think like I used to that you have to wait for some big miracle or big random event in your life to experience an encounter with the Lord or heavenly realms? That is simply not true. The Lord promises that in his word in Hebrews 11:6, for example,

> "But without faith it is impossible to please Him, for he who comes to God must believe that He is, and that He is a rewarder of those who diligently seek Him."

He is a rewarder of those who diligently seek him. Do you know what some of the rewards might be? Sometimes it will be encounters with him! Did you know that people can use all of their human senses in the spiritual things too, like vision, smell, sight, hearing? Some who are used to heavenly encounters exercise the use of all. But some, in the beginning, might use one until they grow into using more. Also, even the daily act of observing his presence or many of the different ways he may communicate a message to you is a skill everyone should develop. I highly recommend a book called, 'The Practice of the Presence of God' by Brother Lawrence. Jesus wants to be down to earth with you. I even invite him to sit in my car on car rides as I talk to him as if a person is sitting there in the seat physically. He may not be physically, but he is spiritually. People forget to invite him and pay attention to him and that he has feelings too! This indeed will help you know that you are not alone. In the following paragraphs, I will share my most recent experiences with you while I teach you the simplicity of walking in the secret place.

There are many events other than the ones I shared with you in this book sprinkled throughout my spiritual young adult hot and cold life. Yes, I was hot and cold and back and forth in my walk. At times profoundly serious in the walk to seek God and at other times lazier. There were times I hungered for God's presence, and other times I was too busy with life. It is true what God's word says

> Do not be deceived, God is not mocked; for whatever a man sows, that he will also reap. For he who sows to his flesh will of the flesh reap corruption, but he who sows to the Spirit will of the Spirit reap everlasting life. And let us not grow weary while doing good, for in due season we shall reap if we do not lose heart.
>
> — GALATIANS 6:7-9

Did you see what that verse says, what will happen if we do not grow weary and lose heart? What will you invest your time, mind, soul, and actions doing? Everlasting life is found only in Jesus and getting to know him is key. When you want to get to know someone, you have to be intentional about making an effort to do so. In my life, that intentionality was good and other times so very lazy. I feel sad at times when I think of the lost precious time I could have had more with my Lord. But I cannot stay in that sadness. He was always waiting for me and has welcomed me into his loving arms each time, and I must, and so should you, focus more on him than what could have, should have been.

Sometimes people make an idol out of their past and mistakes, then the enemy laughs at us, knowing our mind is now off of God's goodness, robbing us our peace that Jesus paid for! In that place in the lack of his Shalom, his peace, we are not fully fulfilling our call. Stop partnering with the enemy who will whisper in your ear all the awful things you have done. Believe me, while I was trying to write this chapter, he attempted to fight my mind again and again, but he is losing the battle! I stood my ground and declared what God's word says I am. I am seated in Heavenly places with Christ Jesus (not Satan) so I told him to shut up and get out in Jesus name!

> and raised us up together and made us sit together in the heavenly places in Christ Jesus.
>
> — EPHESIANS 2:6

We must live from that place here on Earth, knowing we are already seated with him and declaring our God-given authority over this Earth and the dark forces that try to play against you. The dark forces do not want you to live in the freedom Jesus mighty Yeshua paid for if you are a believer. They want you so depressed you're no earthly good to anyone. So, declare

This I recall to my mind, Therefore I have hope. Through the Lord's mercies we are not consumed, Because His compassions fail not. They are new every *morning; Great is Your faithfulness!*

— LAMENTATIONS 3:21- 23

Do you see that his mercies are new every day? He is faithful even if you are not.

You are created to rule and reign, the creepy serpent! Then God said,

> "Let us make man in our image according to Our likeness: let them have dominion over the fish of the sea, over the birds of the air, and over the cattle, over the earth and over every creeping thing that creeps on the earth"

— GENESIS 1:26

So do you remember what happened to Lucifer when he appeared in the garden of Eden to Eve? God made him into a creepy slithering serpent after he tricked Eve to disobey God.

> Behold, I give you the authority to trample on serpents and scorpions, and over all the power of the enemy, and nothing shall by any means hurt you. Nevertheless, do not rejoice in this, that the spirits are subject to you, but rather rejoice because your names are written in heaven."

— LUKE 10:19

You see, we are to walk in the authority given by God to us to be productive for the King of Kings while we are here. The serpent enemy does not rule you. You do not serve him, you serve Jesus. So, we must come to a point where we really live like it and get serious with our maker. He will not force you to, but if you have been bought by the blood of Jesus, there is one thing you can do for him. He says in John 14: 15 *15 "If you love Me, keep My commandments.* So that included ANYTHING he tells you to do also.

"But Susan, how will I know what he has told me to do?"

It comes back to that verse

> And you will seek Me and find Me, when you search for Me with all your heart.
>
> — JEREMIAH 29:13

So right there, he gave you a promise that if you seek him and you will find him, and in that, you will learn to listen to his voice and know what he wants you to do. Be very intentional about seeking him and listening. It is crucial to move from the lazy cold life to the hot on fire, productive, vibrant life with Jesus he wants you to have with him.

So now, back to my original point. Jesus will have encounters with you if you keep pressing into him! This has happened to me. Where you realize it or not at the time he is involved very much so in your life. Now I will tell you of the most recent.

I started attending a class last fall. It was called 'Building With the Spirit" at a wonderful little church. The class taught how to use your senses to hear and see what the Holy Spirit is communicating with you and then partner with what Jesus is telling you to do. One of my experiences as I sat in my car (in my driveway of all places) listening to some Godly messianic worship music Roar In Zion by Paul Wilbur and thinking deeply about my Yeshua. I was feeling so badly yet again of all the wrong choices in the past and yet also feeling so much gratefulness.

You see, sometimes when you are in prayer, or you are, let's say, for example, bowed before God, you actually are. God judges the heart, right? Well, if in your spirit imagination, you are bowing before God, he sees it as such! So, if you are praying and focusing on Jesus and you want to invite him to sit with you in the garden in your spirit's imagination, you can. But I am learning that Jesus, when invited into that secret place with you, longs for it! Sometimes he will take over and show you things! It is amazing. As I said earlier, he is waiting to be invited.

So anyway, I was focused and worshipping, praying, and praising. I kept trying to imagine Jesus sitting beside me in the car and invited him to do so. Well, during all of this, while my eyes were closed, all of a sudden, I saw a vision of me in a beautiful gown. It looked almost like a wedding dress. I saw Jesus as the finest garments. This was beyond my own imagination. I started trying to look at details as best I could in the moment without losing the moment with him. As the music I was listening to played, Jesus grabbed my hand, and we danced together! Like a bride and groom at a wedding. People were around us clapping and smiling and laughing with such joy although I could not make out who they were. We danced, then I saw Jesus step back and clap his hands and stomp his leg like at a country showdown hoedown while he watched me dance a moment solo. He had such a goofy grin of joy. I was totally shocked by this and knew this was beyond my imagination. Jesus had indeed come into the secret place with me when I invited him. We then went to a table that was beautiful with lovely things. Suddenly, a large scroll came out of the table and unrolled in the air right before me. Jesus gave me a large, beautiful quill, and without words, I knew what he was saying.

Neither of us moved our mouths. He motioned for me to sign at the bottom, so I did. The scroll was large and beautiful, and it was edged in gold. That stood out to me. I saw Jesus then sign it, and it rolled up fast and disappeared. I had no idea what I had just signed, but in my heart, I trusted my King Jesus and knew that it was best for me and him to do it together. I was suspecting it was a covenant but was not sure.

We celebrated a bit longer then I was fully back in my car. I was always in my car, but my spirit was indeed with Jesus. You see, over time, He has come to show me that was a renewal of my covenant with Jesus that day. It was a special day for both of us communing together! He knew I was feeling bad often of my guilt of failing him, but he also knew my heart was sick of this sinful earth and its temptations, and he knew I would not ever go back to being cold again, so he gave me a tangible ceremony and new covenant between me and him! But he went on to do more!

A few months after that, I was in class, and we were told to close our eyes and sit with Jesus in a field. Well, and I chuckle as I write this, I did not even get a chance to sit in the field. I was in a vision right away at a pool. I saw Jesus standing there watching me, and yet again, I knew what he was saying to me without him even moving his lips. He wanted me to get in the water and immerse myself. I do not like swimming and cannot swim well. I hate immersing myself in water and putting my head totally under it. I thought surely, I knew he was going to test me on this. So, I thought, *"well, what do I have to lose? I need to face one of my fears. Jesus is standing there watching and waiting to help me if I need,"* I assumed.

So, I quickly got in the pool and immersed myself and obeyed his wanting me to. The pool was pretty simple until I saw on the edge underwater some pretty tile work at eye level when I went under. Then below in the dark, I saw shapes, not knowing what they were and was a little afraid to find out. The water was very thick, and it seemed a little dark in it, yet I could still see. I decided after a few moments to come up, and I saw right away Jesus pacing on the edge of the pool with one hand on his chin watching me, and he told me to go under again. I thought, *"I am not sure why, but ok."* So, I did. Then I came up again after playing a moment in it. I realized the first time I went under I did not have to rush up for air because in heavenly places, it does not matter. So, I came up and saw Jesus there. I had a tiny bit of fear, and he reassured me he was there with me and to go back under. So, I did. This third time was faster, and I came up.

The Pastor of the class said, "Ok class; come back, let's talk about what Jesus showed you."

I had thought Jesus was simply doing an exercise of trust with me to face a fear, but I realized months later, near the Fall Feasts of God in 2020, what actually happened. I had always wondered but never really asked. So, I started asking Jesus what the pool we went to was. Well, one night, I was watching Rabbi Curt Landry, and he was showing a Mikvah pool in a picture at the House of David. He went on to tell the importance of immersion in it. It looked a lot like the pool I saw that Jesus took me too! I knew when I finally asked, not just wondered, that Jesus was showing me what it was!

The Mikvah is very important to the Jews. It is a Jewish ritual bath, a symbol of cleansing and rebirth. For example, the priest would use it prior to performing important duties like on Yom Kippur, the holiest day of the year, the day of atonement.

Jesus took me to a mikvah! I found out that the shapes under the water were indeed stones representing the twelve tribes of Israel that you might find in traditional mikvahs here on earth.

I can, at times, even when I have an encounter with Jesus, I tend to still have some doubt, and I test it. I say, "Jesus, if this was real, please confirm." And as I showed you above, indeed he does. Remember the scroll I signed months prior? The gold edging stood out to me. I wanted confirmation. As soon as I asked, he had me reading a book by Anna Werner, where she described she had seen a scroll with gold edging when with Jesus! I knew I actually was there and saw this! I did not know I would randomly be reading a book by another Christian author and find that small detail that was so important to me.

You see, God's love is so tender, and he truly has the hairs on your head numbered Matthew 10:30! He cares about every detail of you and your heart. Who better to trust it with! Now, will you invite him right now to be with you? Do you trust him right now? Will you allow him to be your Father, Your King, Your best friend, and bridegroom right now? People let you down, and you even let yourself down, but He never will.

Do you long right now to have encounters with him? You can, and he is waiting right now for you. When you do have an encounter with him, be sure to try and see detail, smell if you remember, and feel what it is like. He will speak all sorts of things in each sense to you in the encounter to equip you to partner with creating and building with him stories that will bring him glory. Your story was written before time. Will you partner with what He wrote about you? Do not set your course; those days are over. Let him set the course, RIGHT NOW!

BEFORE YOU GO

Do you want to know how to get back home to God? Just believe in his perfect son, who he sent to die for your sins. John 3:16 *for God so loved the world that he gave his only begotten son, that whoever believes in Him should not perish but have everlasting life.* He made it that simple, but we tend to complicate it. We all are born sinners into a fallen world, but he made a way to get us back home. Accept his son Jesus today and call on his name to come wash your heart and be your savior. He has been waiting for you.

The only way to get to God is by confessing to him, you're a sinner (he will forgive all your sins big & small) and asking forgiveness through the shed blood of Jesus on the cross. We are all sinners, yes, even your friend or relative you thought could do no wrong. *John 3:16 For God so loved the world that he gave his one and only Son, that whoever believes in him shall not perish but have eternal life.* He allowed his son to take your place for what you and the rest of us deserve—to perish forever. Our sin separates us from the Father. Once you're of age to choose Jesus' free gift he is given you, the rest is up to you. He will not force himself on you to accept him or what he did for you. But genuinely think about this:

why on earth would you forfeit such a gift? Why would you waste the blood he shed for your sins to wash you clean in the eyes of God? **Please always remember God loves YOU and you are made in His image.**

Thank you for spending some time with me today reading my book,
I am honored you have. I hope my testimonies shine for his beautiful glory! As I was finishing this book Jesus has already given me the next book topic I am to write, so look for it soon!
Please share this book or my website with someone you think it will bless.
Messengeroftheglory.com
Look for me in Amazon
As Messenger of the Glory series written by Susan D. Jackson

Do you need prayer? Do you have a story to share and allow your story to bring God glory? Did this book help you in some way? Do you have questions?
Email at: MessengeroftheGlory@gmail.com

www.ingramcontent.com/pod-product-compliance
Lightning Source LLC
Chambersburg PA
CBHW071925020426
42331CB00010B/2731